A Study Guide
for
"Joy of the Gospel"
by Pope Francis

Norbert Bufka

A Study Guide for "Joy of the Gospel" by Pope Francis
© Norbert Bufka 2014
No part of this book may be used or reproduced in any manner without written permission of the author, except for brief quotations used in reviews and critiques. All rights reserved.

The author can be contacted by
Email: norbert609@sbcglobal.net
Website: www.thisonly.org.

Evangelii Gaudium(Joy of the Gospel) is copyrighted ©
Libreria Editrice Vaticana, 2013. All rights reserved. Used with permission.

Other books by Norbert Bufka
A Journey to Peace through Justice
Moral Values and Sound Bites
From Bohemia to Good Harbor
News from the Neighborhood
Good Harbor, Michigan

Printed in the United States.

Table of contents

Introduction

This papal document is the easiest one I ever read in terms of the language and flow of the document. It has ordinary language about what it means to be a Christian in its very core. Pope Francis addressed this letter* not only to Catholic leaders but also to the Catholic laity.

Pope Francis wants us to understand that the joy we Christians have is meant to be shared, not in a dogmatic or orthodoxy kind of way, but by living the way Jesus did two millennia ago in befriending those not in power. Jesus' entire life was centered on the poor, the oppressed, and every other category of people who were not in power. It did not matter if they were not Jews. He healed the Roman centurion's trusted servant, even though he was of the despised Roman occupiers. He visited with a Samaritan woman, a practice that was forbidden by Jewish law.

Fr. Hans Küng† wrote this about *Joy of the Gospel*: "Church reform is forging ahead....Pope Francis not only intensifies his criticism of capitalism and the fact that money rules the world, but speaks out clearly in favor of church reform 'at all levels.' He specifically advocates structural reforms -- namely, decentralization toward local dioceses and communities, reform of the papal office, upgrading the laity and against excessive clericalism, in favor of a more effective presence of women in the church, above all in the decision-making bodies. And he comes out equally clearly in favor of ecumenism and interreligious dialogue, especially with Judaism and Islam." [1]

John L. Allen, Jr.‡ wrote, "At the big-picture level, Francis

---

* Technically this is an Apostolic Exhortation.
† Hans Küng (born March 19, 1928) is a Swiss Catholic priest, theologian, and author.

says he wants a more missionary and more merciful church, one less afraid of change than of 'remaining shut up with structures which give us a false sense of security,' 'rules which make us harsh judges,' and 'habits which make us feel safe.'" [2]

I encourage you to read the entire Exhortation. I am writing this little booklet for two reasons: I wish to make the main points of his letter available to more people but more importantly, to add questions and practical comments for you as an individual, or a parish staff person, or even a bishop.

Joy of the Gospel is available in book form at booksellers on line and at stores. You can download it for free from the Vatican website at
http://www.vatican.va/holy_father/francesco/apost_exhortations/ documents/papa-francesco_esortazione-ap_20131124_evangelii-gaudium_en.html

---

[‡] John L. Allen, Jr. (born 1965) is an American journalist who worked for 16 years in Rome as a Vatican watcher, covering news about the Holy See and the Pope.

Prologue

#1-18

Pope Benedict XVI wrote "Being a Christian is not the result of an ethical choice or a lofty idea, but the encounter with an event, a person, which gives life a new horizon and a decisive direction". (#7)[3] Yet many Christians are caught up in consumerism§ and experience "the desolation and anguish born of a complacent yet covetous heart, the feverish pursuit of frivolous pleasures, and a blunted conscience." (#2) As a result they do not experience the joy of the Gospel. Francis calls "all Christians, everywhere, at this very moment, to a renewed personal encounter with Jesus Christ, or at least an openness to letting him encounter them; I ask all of you to do this unfailingly each day." (#3)

Reflection 1

How and when do you encounter Jesus in your life?

Does this encounter challenge you to examine your lifestyle and priorities in regard to buying things?

---

§ a preoccupation with and an inclination toward the buying of consumer goods, especially more than necessary for living a decent life.

The task of evangelization is "communicating life to others. ...An evangelizer must never look like someone who has just come back from a funeral!" (#10) The Holy Spirit must be our guide. (#12) This new evangelization, discussed and promoted in 2012, "is carried out in three principal settings"[4] "the area of ordinary pastoral ministry", "'The baptized whose lives do not reflect the demands of Baptism'[5] who lack a meaningful relationship to the Church", and thirdly "first and foremost about preaching the Gospel to those who do not know Jesus Christ or who have always rejected him." Pope Francis ends this section with these challenging words: ".... "we 'cannot passively and calmly wait in our church buildings'; we need to move 'from a pastoral ministry of mere conservation to a decidedly missionary pastoral ministry'".[6](#15)

Reflection 2

Do you think about how to reach people beyond the borders of the parish and beyond the borders of Catholicism when it comes to serving those in need?

How do you do this?

How does your parish do this?

Pope Francis recognizes that there are many more issues involved in this discussion of evangelization but he does not "believe that the papal magisterium should be expected to offer a definitive or complete word on every question which affects the Church and the world. It is not advisable for the Pope to take the place of local Bishops in the discernment of every issue which arises in their territory. In this sense, I am conscious of the need to promote a sound 'decentralization'".

Reflection 3

This seems to open the door to much local autonomy and initiative to carry out this new evangelization.

What ideas come to mind for you, as a religious, a layperson, a pastor, or a bishop?

Chapter 1 The Church's Missionary Transformation

#19-49

The Great Commission found in Matthew 28:19-20 applied to all the disciples, not just the Apostles. Today that means it applies to the whole People of God, not just the clergy and religious men and women. (#19) The Pope addresses this in five ways. The Church looks outward, not to itself. This begins with examining the Church structure and how pastoral workers envision their roles. These roles have their roots in the heart of the Gospel and have human limitations. He gives us a vision of the Church as "a mother with an open heart".

I. A Church which goes forth

Pope Francis makes this comment about the command to all of us: "God's word is unpredictable in its power....The Church has to accept this unruly freedom of the word, which accomplishes what it wills in ways that surpass our calculations and ways of thinking." (#22)

We can proceed as an evangelizing community because we know God "has taken the initiative … and [we can] stand at the crossroads and welcome the outcast. An evangelizing community gets involved by … touching the suffering flesh of Christ in others. Evangelizers thus take on the 'smell of the sheep' and the sheep are willing to hear their voice." (#24) All of us need to be supportive, enduring, and patient in our evangelization.

Reflection 4

There is a refreshing assurance in the presence and movement of the Holy Spirit in all of our lives.

Do you find this comforting or challenging as a Catholic Christian?

Does this motivate you to go out and touch the suffering and smell the sheep?

II.▯ *Pastoral activity and conversion*

Evangelization must begin with our Church structures so that the structure will enhance and promote our being as an evangelizing community. Pope Francis cautions not to change the structure carelessly but the structure must be imbued with "new life and an authentic evangelical spirit". (#26)

He says an ecclesial renewal cannot be deferred. He is very direct in his comments in this regard: "I dream of a 'missionary option', that is, a missionary impulse capable of transforming everything, so that the Church's customs, ways of doing things, times and schedules, language and structures can be suitably channelled for the evangelization of today's world rather than for her self-preservation." (#27) In #28-31 Pope Francis talks about parish church organization and renewal of the diocese for missionary purposes. He also calls for reform at the highest level by saying "Excessive centralization, rather than proving helpful, complicates the Church's life and her missionary outreach." (#32)

Reflection 5

In light of the above bold direction and your experience of life as a Catholic, how can your parish or diocese become more evangelizing? What reforms are needed at the Vatican (the Curia and the papal office)?

III. From the heart of the Gospel

Pope Francis roots his message in this Exhortation in the Gospel and from there the qualities of love and mercy. While he states the doctrine is important (#33-35) he reminds us at the core of the Gospel "what shines forth is the beauty of the saving love of God made manifest in Jesus Christ who died and rose from the dead." (#36) "What counts above all else is 'faith working through love' (Gal 5:6). Works of love directed to one's neighbour are the most perfect external manifestation of the interior grace of the Spirit." (#37) In external works, "mercy is the greatest of all the virtues." (#37)

Reflection 6

How do you show or experience the virtue of mercy?
What is the relationship between mercy and love?

Preaching must be balanced, Pope Francis tells us. A preacher must not devote his preaching inordinately to his personal or ideological issues. The same imbalance "happens when we speak more about law than about grace, more about the Church than about Christ, more about the Pope than about God's word." (#38) "Before all else, the Gospel invites us to respond to the God of love who saves us, to see God in others and to go forth from ourselves to seek the good of others. Under no circumstance can this invitation be obscured!" (39)

Reflection 7

A key word here is "invitation". How are you inviting others into the love and mercy of God?
Are you more concerned about the law, the Church, and the Pope than about grace, Christ, and God's word?

IV.⬜ *A mission embodied within human limits*

Pope Francis offers a plea and support for diversity. "The Church is herself a missionary disciple; she needs to grow in her interpretation of the revealed word and in her understanding of truth. It is the task of exegetes and theologians to help 'the judgment of the Church to mature'.[7] The other sciences also help to accomplish this, each in its own way….For those who long for a monolithic body of doctrine guarded by all and leaving no room for nuance, this might appear as undesirable and leading to confusion. But in fact such variety serves to bring out and develop different facets of the inexhaustible riches of the Gospel.[8]" (#40)

"Let us never forget that 'the expression of truth can take different forms.'" (#41) Customs must be evaluated in light of current understanding and discarded freely so as not to hamper the Gospel. (#43) "…the confessional must not be a torture chamber but rather an encounter with the Lord's mercy which spurs us on to do our best." (#44) "…the task of evangelization operates within the limits of language and of circumstances." (#45)

Reflection 8

Pope Francis is very blunt here about diversity of interpretation of truths and he also insists on pastoral care that flows from mercy and love, not doctrine, dogma, and rules. How do these ideas mesh with your role as a member of the Church and disciple of Jesus?

V. A mother with an open heart

Pope Francis calls us to be like a mother with an open heart. "The Church is called to be the house of the Father, with doors always wide open. One concrete sign of such openness is that our church doors should always be open, so that if someone, moved by the Spirit, comes there looking for God, he or she will not find a closed door. There are other doors that should not be closed either. Everyone can share in some way in the life of the Church; everyone can be part of the community, nor should the doors of the sacraments be closed for simply any reason. This is especially true of the sacrament which is itself 'the door': baptism. The Eucharist, although it is the fullness of sacramental life, is not a prize for the perfect but a powerful medicine and nourishment for the weak.[9] These convictions have pastoral consequences that we are called to consider with prudence and boldness. Frequently, we act as arbiters of grace rather than its facilitators. But the Church is not a tollhouse; it is the house of the Father, where there is a place for everyone, with all their problems." (#47)

He tells us we need to go to the poor first, not our friends and the rich. (#48) He wants "a Church which is bruised, hurting and dirty because it has been out on the streets, rather than a Church which is unhealthy from being confined and from clinging to its own security." (#49)

Reflection 9

Can we really keep the church doors open? What are the implications of open doors, not only for the physical building but being more inviting to people in celebrating the sacraments?

Do you enjoy the mercy of God when you celebrate the sacrament of reconciliation?

Do you feel invited to the Eucharistic table? As a staff person or member of the clergy, do you encourage people to participate or hold up the rules to keep them out?

How can you think outside the rules?

Chapter 2 Amid The Crisis Of Communal Commitment

#50-109

Pope Francis begins with an exhortation to an "ever watchful scrutiny of the signs of the times". (#51) He sees two areas of major concern in this regard: challenges of today's world and temptations faced by pastoral workers.

I. Some challenges of today's world

Some of the challenges are an economy of exclusion brought on by trickle-down economics (#54), the new "idolatry of money" and a "deified market"(#55 and 56), a financial system that rules rather than serves (#57 and 58), and inequality which spawns violence (#59).

Pope Francis is very critical of the free market economy that is held in very high regard by some people. He wrote, "a sage in antiquity said 'Not to share one's wealth with the poor is to steal from them and to take away their livelihood. It is not our own goods which we hold, but theirs'".[10] (#57) "….the rich must help, respect and promote the poor." (#58) "…. until exclusion and inequality in society and between peoples are reversed, it will be impossible to eliminate violence." (#59)

Reflection 10

Is your first reaction to these comments one of support or rejection?

In either case, what steps can you take to change the reverence given to the free market? What can you do to help the poor?

What is the Pope asking rich people to do?

How can you apply this to your own life?

What is the pope asking parishes and dioceses to do in the above situations?

What steps do you need to take to reverse the worship of the market in our society?

_____

Next, Pope Francis speaks of some cultural challenges that keep us from helping the poor. When one holds too tightly to one's own truth, "it becomes difficult for citizens to devise a common plan which transcends individual gain and personal ambitions." (#61) Globalization and other factors are destroying cultures without offering anything better. Fundamentalism and no God spirituality are not solutions to problems. Secularization and moral relativism tear down moral values. Families face serious challenges. (#63-67)

The challenge to enculturating our faith can be met by an "authentic Christian humanism." (#68) "Houses and neighbourhoods are more often built to isolate and protect than to connect and integrate." (#75)

Reflection 11

Are these cultural challenges part of your life? How can you as an individual overcome these challenges that keep us from sharing the good news of God's love and mercy?

II.￼ *Temptations faced by pastoral workers*

Pope Francis wrote that pastoral workers** must be

recognized and supported so they don't burn out in their ministry. They can be healed by sharing their stories. (#76-77)

Pastoral workers need to and can develop a missionary spirituality. Pope Francis says that " heightened individualism, a crisis of identity and a cooling of fervor … are three evils which fuel one another" and weaken pastoral ministry. (#78) Cynicism tears down the pastoral care workers and practical relativism is worse than doctrinal relativism. (#79 and 80) Too many pastoral workers guard their free time more than evangelization and are obsessed with immediate results. (#81 and 82) We must say no to sterile pessimism and defeatism which are very prevalent in our world. Faith and hope, hallmarks of being Christian, can overcome these evils.   (#85 and 86)

Reflection 12

Have you ever been burned out in your ministry?

Have you thought of the reasons why?

Have you shared these with your pastor?

Have you felt supported in your ministry? Have you conveyed this to your pastor?

How are you and your parish affected by "sterile pessimism" and "defeatism".?

"Isolation, which is a version of immanentism, can find expression in a false autonomy which has no place for God. But in the realm of religion it can also take the form of a spiritual consumerism tailored to one's own unhealthy individualism. The

---

** Pastoral workers are all clergy and religious men and women as well as all lay people who reach out not only to others in our Church but to others in the wider community. Examples are lectors, ministers to the homebound, workers in soup kitchens.

return to the sacred and the quest for spirituality which mark our own time are ambiguous phenomena. Today, our challenge is not so much atheism as the need to respond adequately to many people's thirst for God, lest they try to satisfy it with alienating solutions or with a disembodied Jesus who demands nothing of us with regard to others. Unless these people find in the Church a spirituality which can offer healing and liberation, and fill them with life and peace, while at the same time summoning them to fraternal communion and missionary fruitfulness, they will end up by being taken in by solutions which neither make life truly human nor give glory to God." (#89)

"The solution will never be found in fleeing from a personal and committed relationship with God which at the same time commits us to serving others." (#91)

Reflection 13

Do you know people who are thirsting for God?
Have you shared your experience of God with them?

Pope Francis has some very strong words against what he calls "spiritual worldliness". First in this category are those who hold on to the past. (#94)

Some people, he wrote, have "an ostentatious preoccupation for the liturgy, for doctrine and for the Church's prestige" with little or no care for the needs of the people. As a result the "life of the Church" becomes a "museum piece" and "the property of a select few." Others are fascinated "with social and political gain" or obsessed with "programs of self-help" or are concerned about appearances or caught up in business administration "whose principal beneficiary is not God's people but the Church as an institution….Closed and elite groups are formed" to satisfy their own needs and not the needs of God and God's people.

(#95)

This spiritual worldliness leads us to "indulge in endless fantasies and we lose contact with the real lives and difficulties of our people." (#96)

"Their hearts are open only to the limited horizon of their own immanence and interests....This is a tremendous corruption disguised as a good. We need to avoid it by making the Church constantly go out from herself, keeping her mission focused on Jesus Christ, and her commitment to the poor. God save us from a worldly Church with superficial spiritual and pastoral trappings! This stifling worldliness can only be healed by breathing in the pure air of the Holy Spirit.... Let us not allow ourselves to be robbed of the Gospel!" (#97)

Reflection 14

How are you as a pastor making the "life of the Church" " ... "a "museum piece" and "the property of a select few"?

Pope Francis has mentioned the Holy Spirit several times. Do you experience the refreshing breath of the Holy Spirit in your daily life and in your ministry?

We must stop fighting among ourselves by ending exclusivist groups (#98) and resisting divisions (#99) with love (#100). "To pray for a person with whom I am irritated is a beautiful step forward in love, and an act of evangelization. Let us do it today! Let us not allow ourselves to be robbed of the ideal of fraternal love!" (#101)

Reflection 15

Do you find yourself in a group that excludes others?

Do you welcome others who are different than you in some way?

16

Other challenges of the church involve the laity. "Lay people are, put simply, the vast majority of the people of God. The minority – ordained ministers – are at their service." Pope Francis praises lay ministry and criticizes "excessive clericalism". (#102)

"But we need to create still broader opportunities for a more incisive female presence in the Church". Because 'the feminine genius is needed in all expressions in the life of society, the presence of women must also be guaranteed in the workplace'[11] and in the various other settings where important decisions are made, both in the Church and in social structures." (#103)

"Demands that the legitimate rights of women be respected, based on the firm conviction that men and women are equal in dignity, present the Church with profound and challenging questions which cannot be lightly evaded. The reservation of the priesthood to males, as a sign of Christ the Spouse who gives himself in the Eucharist, is not a question open to discussion, but it can prove especially divisive if sacramental power is too closely identified with power in general. It must be remembered that when we speak of sacramental power 'we are in the realm of function, not that of dignity or holiness'[12]. The ministerial priesthood is one means employed by Jesus for the service of his people, yet our great dignity derives from baptism, which is accessible to all. The configuration of the priest to Christ the head – namely, as the principal source of grace – does not imply an exaltation which would set him above others. In the Church, functions 'do not favour the superiority of some vis-à-vis the others'.[13] Indeed, a woman, Mary, is more important than the bishops. Even when the function of ministerial priesthood is considered 'hierarchical', it must be remembered that 'it is totally ordered to the holiness of Christ's members'.[14] Its key and axis is not power understood as domination, but the power to administer the sacrament of the Eucharist; this is the origin of its authority, which is always a service to God's people. This presents a great challenge for pastors and theologians, who are in a position to recognize more fully what this entails with regard to the possible role of women in decision-making in different areas of the Church's life." (#104)

Pope Francis wrote briefly on youth ministry and faith formation. (#105)

Shortage of priestly and religious vocations "is often due to a lack of contagious apostolic fervour in communities which results in a cooling of enthusiasm and attractiveness." We cannot accept all candidates for priesthood especially if they are seeking prestige, power, or security. (#107)

Reflection 16

While Pope Francis clearly upholds the ordination of men only, he seems to be open to raising the role of women in the Church to a level as close to ordination as possible.

What are your thoughts on Pope Francis' words and my comment?

Do you think "prestige, power, or security" are good qualities in a priest?

Chapter 3 The Proclamation of the Gospel

#110-175

"'…. evangelization as the joyful, patient and progressive preaching of the saving death and resurrection of Jesus Christ must be your absolute priority.'"[15] (#110) Pope Francis speaks to all of us in the first part of this chapter and then specifically addresses preaching the homily.

I. The entire people of God proclaims the Gospel

"The salvation which God offers us is the work of his mercy….No one is saved by himself or herself, individually, or by his or her own efforts.…The Church must be a place of mercy freely given, where everyone can feel welcomed, loved, forgiven and encouraged to live the good life of the Gospel." (#112-114)

"Grace supposes culture, and God's gift becomes flesh in the culture of those who receive it.….'every culture offers positive values and forms which can enrich the way the Gospel is preached, understood and lived.'[16] …. It is an indisputable fact that no single culture can exhaust the mystery of our redemption in Christ." (#115-118)

Reflection 17

Pope Francis is very clear on the nature of salvation as a community event, not just a personal one.

How do you mesh with the community of believers?

Do you accept people who are "different" in some way from you as part of this community? Do you mentally exclude anyone for any reason? How can you overcome this exclusionary thinking?

Salvation is an act of God's mercy, not an earned benefit, the pope wrote. Yet our liturgy is filled with words like merit, reward, and earning salvation. How do you reconcile these apparent contradictory views?

Pope Francis says we are all missionary disciples. "The new evangelization calls for personal involvement on the part of each of the baptized" and "each of us should find ways to communicate Jesus wherever we are." (#120-121)

Person to person evangelization "is the informal preaching which takes place in the middle of a conversation....In this preaching, which is always respectful and gentle, the first step is personal dialogue, when the other person speaks and shares his or her joys, hopes and concerns for loved ones, or so many other heartfelt needs....We should not think, however, that the Gospel message must always be communicated by fixed formulations learned by heart or by specific words which express an absolutely invariable content." (#127-129)

Reflection 18

Have you thought of personal conversations as a form of evangelization?

How can you make this a more positive focus for you at school, at work, at church, and in the larger community?

"The Holy Spirit also enriches the entire evangelizing Church with different charisms.[††] These gifts are meant to renew and build up the Church.[17] They are not an inheritance, safely

[††] A charism is a talent or gift that flows from the love of God in that person's life.

secured and entrusted to a small group for safekeeping; rather they are gifts of the Spirit integrated into the body of the Church, drawn to the centre which is Christ and then channelled into an evangelizing impulse. A sure sign of the authenticity of a charism is its ecclesial character, its ability to be integrated harmoniously into the life of God's holy and faithful people for the good of all. Something truly new brought about by the Spirit need not overshadow other gifts and spiritualities in making itself felt. To the extent that a charism is better directed to the heart of the Gospel, its exercise will be more ecclesial. It is in communion, even when this proves painful, that a charism is seen to be authentic and mysteriously fruitful. On the basis of her response to this challenge, the Church can be a model of peace in our world." (#130) "whenever we attempt to create unity on the basis of our human calculations, we end up imposing a monolithic uniformity. This is not helpful for the Church's mission." (#131) Theologians and scientists have much to offer. (#133)

Reflection 19

How can you use your talents to evangelize, i.e. to spread the love and mercy of God in your community?

How can you use your talents to mesh with others?

If you are a scientist or a person with special expertise, have you thought of using these talents for the benefit of the Gospel?

As pastor or bishop, do you encourage the people to accept the work of the Holy Spirit in their lives?

Reflect on your parish and the wider church in regard to what is unity and what is conformity.

II. The homily[‡‡]

"The homily is the touchstone for judging a pastor's closeness and ability to communicate to his people." (#135) "The preacher must know the heart of his community, in order to realize where its desire for God is alive and ardent, as well as where that dialogue, once loving, has been thwarted and is now barren." (#137) "This context demands that preaching should guide the assembly, and the preacher, to a life-changing communion with Christ in the Eucharist. This means that the words of the preacher must be measured, so that the Lord, more than his minister, will be the center of attention." (#138) A preacher must have the same concern and love for the people as a mother has for her children. (#139-140)

Reflection 20

If you are a preacher, do you think about this ideal when preparing and giving a homily?

Is your focus on the Word?

If not a preacher, do the homilies you hear reflect this ideal?

If not, have you lovingly given feedback to the preacher?

Dialog is a communication between two or more people by using words. If done in a respectful manner it helps each participant become a better person. "A preaching which would be purely moralistic or doctrinaire, or one which turns into a lecture on biblical exegesis, detracts from this heart-to-heart

[‡‡] A homily is the sharing of the meaning of the Scripture readings at Mass or some other liturgy. While only an ordained person can can give a homily, there are occasions when other people may share a reflection on the Scripture. It seems fitting that these words of Pope Francis apply to those kinds of talks as well.

communication which takes place in the homily and possesses a quasi-sacramental character: 'Faith comes from what is heard, and what is heard comes by the preaching of Christ' (Rom 10:17).'" Truth goes hand in hand with beauty through the images that are used in the homily so that the hearer "will sense that each word of Scripture is a gift before it is a demand." (#142)

Reflection 21

Does your preaching involve images that convey the love of God rather than abstract truths?

Have you asked for regular feedback on your homilies?

III. Preparing to preach

"A preacher who does not prepare is not 'spiritual'; he is dishonest and irresponsible with the gifts he has received." (#145) Preachers must take time to reflect on the scriptures being preached about. Personalizing the word, spiritual reading, having an ear to the people, and using homiletic resources are all helpful in preparing to give a good homily. (#143 -149)

Reflection 22

Do you take an appropriate time and use resources to reflect on the readings prior to preaching?

What would make you a better preacher?

IV.⬚ *Evangelization and the deeper understanding of the kerygma*

Kerygma is the first proclamation that God loves you. (#160) The Great Commission is a mandate to help people experience the love of God and know that Jesus loves them. It calls us to grow in faith. (#160) The basis for Jesus' moral mandate is "This is my commandment, that you love one another as I have loved you" (Jn 15:12). (#161) Growth in faith is nurtured by education and catechesis. (#163) "Listening, in communication, is an openness of heart which makes possible that closeness without which genuine spiritual encounter cannot occur. Listening helps us to find the right gesture and word which shows that we are more than simply bystanders." (#171)

"The sacred Scriptures are the very source of evangelization. Consequently, we need to be constantly trained in hearing the word." (#174) "Evangelization demands familiarity with God's word, which calls for dioceses, parishes and Catholic associations to provide for a serious, ongoing study of the Bible, while encouraging its prayerful individual and communal reading.[18] We do not blindly seek God, or wait for him to speak to us first, for 'God has already spoken, and there is nothing further that we need to know, which has not been revealed to us'.[19] "Let us receive the sublime treasure of the revealed word." (#175)

Reflection 23

How often do you read and study the scriptures?

Do you have a daily time to do this or is it when the spirit moves you?

Chapter 4 The Social Dimension Of Evangelization

#176-258

In this chapter Pope Francis deals with the "concerns about the social dimension of evangelization" (#176) These include "communal and societal repercussions of the kerygma", "the inclusion of the poor in society", "the common good and peace in society", and "social dialogue as a contribution to peace".

I. Communal and societal repercussions of the kerygma

"To believe that the Son of God assumed our human flesh means that each human person has been taken up into the very heart of God" through " liberating work of the Spirit…" (#177) The challenge of the kingdom can be summed up as follows: "'Seek first God's kingdom and his righteousness, and all these things will be given to you as well' (Mt 6:33). Jesus' mission is to inaugurate the kingdom of his Father; he commands his disciples to proclaim the good news that 'the kingdom of heaven is at hand'(Mt 10:7)". (#180)

"An authentic faith – which is never comfortable or completely personal – always involves a deep desire to change the world, to transmit values, to leave this earth somehow better than we found it." (#183) This gives the challenge of the kingdom a profound social dimension but "neither the Pope nor the Church have a monopoly on the interpretation of social realities or the proposal of solutions to contemporary problems." (#184)

Reflection 24

Do you feel you have been "taken up into the very heart of God"?

What does Pope Francis mean that "authentic faith" is never comfortable?

The Pope says that faith "always involves a deep desire to

change the world." Is this your experience? If not, what do you need to change?

II. The inclusion of the poor in society

"Each individual Christian and every community is called to be an instrument of God for the liberation and promotion of the poor, and for enabling them to be fully a part of society.…'How does God's love abide in anyone who has the world's goods, and sees a brother or sister in need and yet refuses help?' (1 Jn 3:17)". (#187)

" [Solidarity] presumes the creation of a new mindset which thinks in terms of community and the priority of the life of all over the appropriation of goods by a few." (#188)

In regard to helping the poor, "we are not simply talking about ensuring nourishment or a 'dignified sustenance' for all people, but also their 'general temporal welfare and prosperity'.[20] This means education, access to health care, and above all employment, for it is through free, creative, participatory and mutually supportive labor that human beings express and enhance the dignity of their lives. A just wage enables them to have adequate access to all the other goods which are destined for our common use." (192) Let's heed the simple command of God's word to care for the poor. (#194)

Reflection 25

Do you have a plan to help someone in need? Do you advocate for the poor?

Does your parish and diocese actively seek ways to assist the poor?

Perhaps it would be good at this point to identify the poor in your community. In what ways are they poor? (Pope Francis mentions several areas in #192.)

The special place of the poor in God's people calls us to have a preferential option for the poor and be evangelized by them. (#198) God calls us to not merely activism but to attentiveness to the poor. (#199) The worst discrimination is the lack of spiritual care. (#200) Pope Francis concludes with "I trust in the openness and readiness of all Christians, and I ask you to seek, as a community, creative ways of accepting this renewed call" to heed the preferential option for the poor. (#201)

Reflection 26

Are you "ready" to find creative ways to make the "preferential option for the poor" a reality in your parish and diocese?

In looking at the root problem of why people are poor, Francis says, "As long as the problems of the poor are not radically resolved by rejecting the absolute autonomy of markets and financial speculation and by attacking the structural causes of inequality,[21] no solution will be found for the world's problems or, for that matter, to any problems. Inequality is the root of social ills." (#202)

"Business is a vocation, and a noble vocation, provided that those engaged in it see themselves challenged by a greater meaning in life; this will enable them truly to serve the common

28

good by striving to increase the goods of this world and to make them more accessible to all." (#203)

"The economy can no longer turn to remedies that are a new poison, such as attempting to increase profits by reducing the work force and thereby adding to the ranks of the excluded." (#204) The Pope appeals to politicians to seek the common good (#205) and we need a better way of interacting among nations. (#206) Too many church communities have no regard for the poor. (#207)

Reflection 27

To tackle the systemic causes of poverty requires significant effort.

Are you willing to accept that challenge?

Are you ready to view social ills through the lens of the common good?

Pope Francis concludes this section with concern for the vulnerable: Regarding human trafficking, he said, "There is greater complicity than we think. The issue involves everyone! This infamous network of crime is now well established in our cities, and many people have blood on their hands as a result of their comfortable and silent complicity." (#211)

Women and unborn children are vulnerable. (#212 and 213) We have ignored the cry of women in desperate situations that lead them to abortion. (#214) Finally, we have exploited nature. (#215)

Reflection 28

The Pope seems to be saying that we are all "complicit" in human trafficking and the number of abortions because we fail to see people in need of care of some kind or we just pass on by.

How are you complicit?

III. *The common good and peace in society*

"The dignity of the human person and the common good rank higher than the comfort of those who refuse to renounce their privileges. When these values are threatened, a prophetic voice must be raised." (#218) He outlines four paths to peace. (#221)

Reflection 29

How can you be a prophetic voice for the common good?

There is a tension between fullness and limitation. (#222) "In the midst of conflict, we lose our sense of the profound unity of reality." (#226)

"…the best way to deal with conflict … is the willingness to face conflict head on, to resolve it and to make it a link in the chain of a new process. 'Blessed are the peacemakers' (Mt 5:9)." (#227) "… unity is greater than conflict." (228)

The pope wrote that realities are more important than ideas, but there is a tension between ideas and reality. There is a tension between the global and the local because the whole is greater than the parts but it is also greater than the sum of its parts.

Reflection 30

Are you willing to face conflict?
Are you able to maintain your cool in a conflict and

30

remember that there is fundamental unity?

IV. Social dialogue as a contribution to peace

"Evangelization also involves the path of dialogue. For the Church today, three areas of dialogue stand out where she needs to be present in order to promote full human development and to pursue the common good: dialogue with states, dialogue with society – including dialogue with cultures and the sciences – and dialogue with other believers who are not part of the Catholic Church." (#238)

"Whenever the sciences – rigorously focused on their specific field of inquiry – arrive at a conclusion which reason cannot refute, faith does not contradict it." (#243)

"We must never forget that we are pilgrims journeying alongside one another. This means that we must have sincere trust in our fellow pilgrims," (#244)

The pope encourages dialog with the Jews, who have not lost their covenant with God. (#247) "Evangelization and interreligious dialogue, far from being opposed, mutually support and nourish one another.[22]" (#251) Pope Francis reminds us that Muslims worship the God of Abraham, as do we Christians. (#253) and we must maintain a dialog with non-Christians as well. (#254)

"The respect due to the agnostic or non-believing minority should not be arbitrarily imposed in a way that silences the convictions of the believing majority or ignores the wealth of religious traditions." (#255)

Pope Francis concludes this chapter with these words: "Starting from certain social issues of great importance for the future of humanity, I have tried to make explicit once again the inescapable social dimension of the Gospel message and to encourage all Christians to demonstrate it by their words, attitudes and deeds." (#258)

Reflection 31

Do you recognize the Jews, non-Catholics, and all people as fellow pilgrims?

Do you have dialog with them?

Chapter 5 Spirit-Filled Evangelizers

#259-288

"Spirit-filled evangelizers means evangelizers fearlessly open to the working of the Holy Spirit. At Pentecost, the Spirit made the apostles go forth from themselves and turned them into heralds of God's wondrous deeds, capable of speaking to each person in his or her own language. The Holy Spirit also grants the courage to proclaim the newness of the Gospel with boldness (parrhesía) in every time and place, even when it meets with opposition. Let us call upon him today, firmly rooted in prayer, for without prayer all our activity risks being fruitless and our message empty. Jesus wants evangelizers who proclaim the good news not only with words, but above all by a life transfigured by God's presence." (#259) Briefly put, "A spirit-filled evangelization is one guided by the Holy Spirit." (#261)

Reflection 32

Are you ready to have the Spirit guide you in evangelistic ministry?

I. Reasons for a renewed missionary impulse

"Without prolonged moments of adoration, of prayerful encounter with the word, of sincere conversation with the Lord, our work easily becomes meaningless; we lose energy as a result of weariness and difficulties, and our fervour dies out…. a privatized lifestyle can lead Christians to take refuge in some false forms of spirituality." (#262)

"The best incentive for sharing the Gospel comes from contemplating it with love, lingering over its pages and reading it with the heart." (#264) "We have a treasure of life and love which cannot deceive, and a message which cannot mislead or disappoint." (#265) "But this conviction has to be sustained by our own constantly renewed experience of savoring Christ's friendship and his message." (#266)

Reflection 33

How is your prayer life helping you to strengthen the faith and share it with others?

"Mission is at once a passion for Jesus and a passion for his people." (#268) "Sometimes we are tempted to be that kind of Christian who keeps the Lord's wounds at arm's length. Yet Jesus wants us to touch human misery, to touch the suffering flesh of others. He hopes that we will stop looking for those personal or communal niches which shelter us from the maelstrom of human misfortune and instead enter into the reality of other people's lives and know the power of tenderness. Whenever we do so, our lives become wonderfully complicated and we experience intensely what it is to be a people, to be part of a people." (#270) "When we live out a spirituality of drawing nearer to others and seeking their welfare, our hearts are opened wide to the Lord's greatest and most beautiful gifts." (#272)

There is a mysterious working of the risen Christ and his Spirit. Trust in God to produce results, but don't expect to see them. Don't count the number of people who come but rather the seed that is sown. (#279) Trust in the Holy Spirit and let him guide wherever he wants us to go. (#281) There is resurrection every day.

Reflection 34

Are you willing to take the risk of being with the wounded and experience the love of God through them?

Can you let go of the very human need to see results of your ministry?

Can you let the Spirit work through you?

II. *Mary, mother of evangelization*

Jesus' gift to his people is Mary, who is a model for evangelization. (#285) She is our mother and the mother of the Church.

Reflection 35

Do you find in Mary a source of comfort in the struggles of life?

Suggestions for groups

Decide when and where to meet as well as beginning and ending time. Times are very important when all are so very busy. A home is ideal for group discussions as it is a warm and comfortable place. Snacks and beverages can distract from the purpose of these meetings so they should be kept to a minimum.

Choose a facilitator for all the sessions or rotate that responsibility if one has not already been designated. A facilitator guides the discussion and helps people follow the guidelines below. It is good to begin and end with prayer. It can be as simple as calling on the Holy Spirit to open your hearts and close with the Our Father.

It is suggested that there be six sessions. The first session will be for all to introduce themselves and agree to the Group Guidelines below. If someone does not agree, find a way to reword it and agree. These are important to build trust. If more than one person will facilitate sessions, determine that at this meeting. Also select a recorder who will write down all the important comments and suggestions that come up. These will be reviewed in the last session. If the participants have the book in advance, then discuss the Introduction and Prologue as well. Otherwise go over them in the second session with Chapter 1.

The next sessions follow the chapters in the book. The last session will involve summarizing the key points as written by the recorder. The group then will choose those for which there is consensus and the group will designate someone to take them to the pastor or bishop, depending on the origin of your group.

Group Guidelines

As a gift to others and to myself in this group, I will share in the responsibility of maintaining a trusting and vibrant group. Specifically, I will do my best to live the following guidelines in participating in this group:

1. I will come prepared to each session.
2. I will not miss sessions, except for emergencies, since the life of the group depends on each of us being present to one another.
3. I will share who I am with others, expressing my thoughts and opinions, and feelings honestly with others in the group, as appropriate to the topic. I will do this by using "I" rather than "we" or "you" statements.
4. I will listen to others without trying to give advice; I will respect differences of opinions without insisting that others agree with my position.
5. I will maintain the confidentiality of the group; I will not repeat outside of this group the personal information I hear within this group.
6. I will encourage others to go deeper in their understanding of what has been shared; I will support them in their searching.
7. I will help to make sure that everyone who wants to speak has an opportunity to speak within the group.
8. I promise not only support for the others, but expression of that support as well.
9. I will express ideas in concrete and specific terms as much as possible.

These guidelines are based on the book, *Facilitating for Growth* by Barbara Fleischer.

Endnotes

---

[1] Hans Kung, "Church reform at all levels", *NCROnline*, December 2, 2013.
   http://ncronline.org/news/vatican/church-reform-all-levels
[2] John L. Allen, "Francis and a church that breathes with both lungs", *NCROnline*, November 27, 2013.
http://ncronline.org/node/65121
[3] [3] Encyclical Letter Deus Caritas Est (25 December 2005), 1: AAS 98 (2006), 217.
[4] [10] Cf. Propositio 7.
[5] [11] Benedict XVI, Homily at Mass for the Conclusion of the Synod of Bishops (28 October 2012): AAS 104 (2102), 890.
[6] [17] Fifth general conference of the latin american and caribbean bishops, Aparecida Document, 29 June 2007, 548 and 370
[7] [42] Second Vatican Ecumenical Council, Dogmatic Constitution on Divine Revelation Dei Verbum, 12.
[8] [44] Saint Thomas Aquinas noted that the multiplicity and variety "were the intention of the first agent", who wished that "what each individual thing lacked in order to reflect the divine goodness would be made up for by other things", since the Creator's goodness "could not be fittingly reflected by just one creature" (S. Th., I, q. 47, a. 1). Consequently, we need to grasp the variety of things in their multiple relationships (cf. S. Th., I, q. 47, a. 2, ad 1; q. 47, a. 3). By analogy, we need to listen to and complement one another in our partial reception of reality and the Gospel.
[9] [51] Cf. Saint Ambrose, De Sacramentis, IV, 6, 28: PL 16, 464: "I must receive it always, so that it may always forgive

my sins. If I sin continually, I must always have a remedy"; ID., op. cit., IV, 5, 24: PL 16, 463: "Those who ate manna died; those who eat this body will obtain the forgiveness of their sins"; Saint Cyril of Alexandria, In Joh. Evang., IV, 2: PG 73, 584-585: "I examined myself and I found myself unworthy. To those who speak thus I say: when will you be worthy? When at last you present yourself before Christ? And if your sins prevent you from drawing nigh, and you never cease to fall – for, as the Psalm says, 'what man knows his faults?' – will you remain without partaking of the sanctification that gives life for eternity?"

[10] [55] Saint John Chrysostom, De Lazaro Concio, II, 6: PG 48, 992D.

[11] [72] Pontifical Council for Justice and Peace, Compendium of the Social Doctrine of the Church, 295.

[12] [73] John Paul II, Post-Synodal Apostolic Exhortation Christifideles Laici (30 December 1988), 51: AAS 81 (1989), 413.

[13] [74] Congregation for the Doctrine of the Faith, Declaration Inter Insigniores on the Question of the Admission of Women to the Ministerial Priesthood (15 October 1976): AAS 68 (1977) 115, cited in John Paul II, Post-Synodal Apostolic Exhortation Christifideles Laici (30 December 1988), note 190: AAS 81 (1989), 493.

[14] [75] John Paul II, Apostolic Letter Mulieris Dignitatem (15 August 1988), 27: AAS 80 (1988), 1718.

[15] [77] John Paul II, Post-Synodal Apostolic Exhortation Ecclesia in Asia (6 November 1999), 19: AAS 92 (2000), 478.

[78] Ibid, 2: AAS 92 (2000), 451.

[16] [91] John Paul II, Post-Synodal Apostolic Exhortation Ecclesia in Oceania (22 November 2001), 16: AAS 94 (2002), 383.

[17] [108] Cf. Second Vatican Ecumenical Council, Dogmatic Constitution on the Church Lumen Gentium, 12.

[18] [138] Cf. Benedict XVI, Post-Synodal Apostolic Exhortation Verbum Domini (30 September 2010), 86-87: AAS 102 (2010), 757-760.

[19] [139] Benedict XVI, Address during the First General Congregation of the Synod of Bishops (8 October 2012): AAS 104 (2012), 896.

[20] [159] John XIII, Encyclical Letter Mater et Magistra (15 May 1961), 3: AAS 53 (1961), 402.

[21] [173] This implies a commitment to "eliminate the structural causes of global economic dysfunction": Benedict XVI, Address to the Diplomatic Corps (8 January 2007): AAS 99 (2007), 73.

[22] [197] Cf. Benedict XVI, Address to the Roman Curia (21 December 2012): AAS 105 (2006), 51; Second Vatican Ecumenical Council, Decree on the Missionary Activity of the Church Ad Gentes, 9; Catechism of the Catholic Church, 856.

Made in the USA
San Bernardino, CA
04 July 2014